D'Nealian™ Handwriting

Author: Donald N. Thurber

Adviser: Dale R. Jordan

Consultant: Verda Krabbe

Scott, Foresman and Company
Editorial Offices: Glenview, Illinois

Regional Sales Offices: Palo Alto, California •
Tucker, Georgia • Glenview, Illinois •
Oakland, New Jersey • Dallas, Texas

Contents

ISBN: 0-673-11520-8

Copyright © 1978.
Scott, Foresman and Company, Glenview, Illinois.
All Rights Reserved.
Printed in the United States of America.

2345678910-WEB-8584838281807978

D'Nealian Handwriting, Book 1. © Scott, Foresman and Company.

Dear Family,

This year your child will be using the D'Nealian Handwriting Program. Our main goal is to help your child learn to write legibly.

Most lower-case or small letters are written with one continuous stroke. Therefore, your child should not lift the pencil from the paper, except when writing a letter that has a cross stroke or a dot.

For your convenience, the D'Nealian letters and numbers are printed on the back of this sheet. The arrows on the letters and numbers show the directions for the strokes.

When helping your child write, we encourage you to use the D'Nealian alphabet and numbers.

Sincerely,

0 1 2 3 4 5 6 7 8 9 10

a b c d e f g h i

j k l m n o p q r

s t u v w x y z

A B C D E F G H I

J K L M N O P Q R

S T U V W X Y Z

D'Nealian Handwriting, Book 1. © Scott, Foresman and Company.

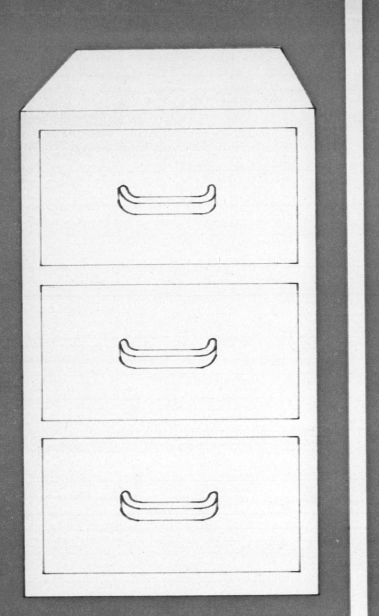

name _____

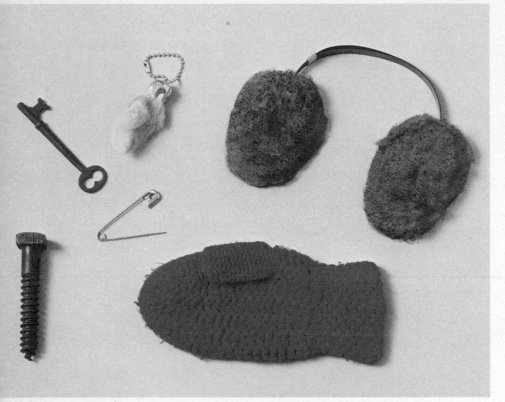

name _____

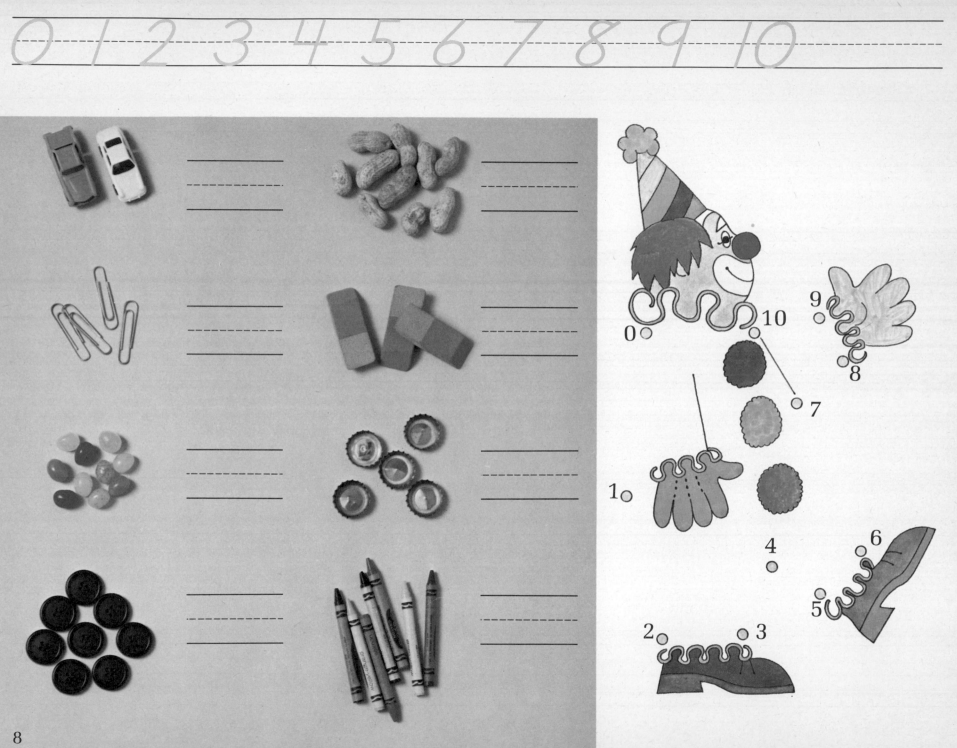

l	t	l	i	H	A	I	H
m	m	n	x	R	R	P	K
r	b	r	o	U	V	U	Y

name _____

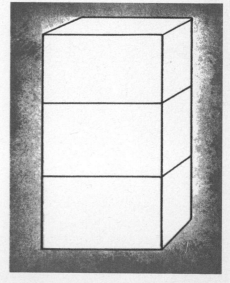

D'Nealian Handwriting, Book 1. © Scott, Foresman and Company.

13

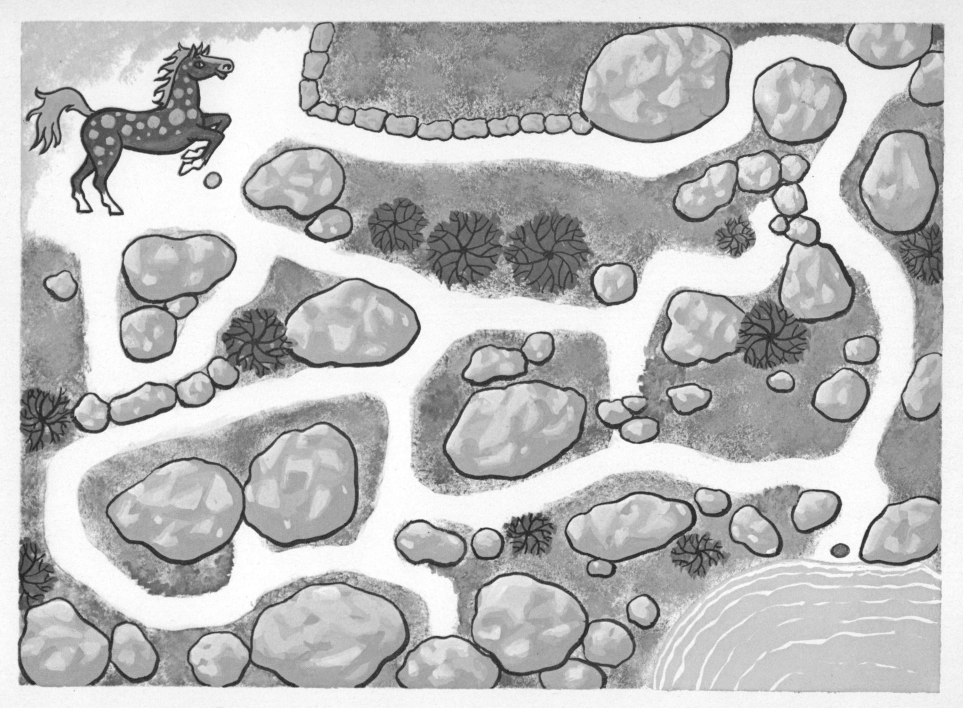

14

0 1 2 3 4 5 6 7 8 9 10

f l f t t T H T I

e e s a N A M N

q y g q B B P R

16

D'Nealian Handwriting, Book 1. © Scott, Foresman and Company.

alligator   bananas   umbrella

ā a a a ā a a   a

a   a

a   a

name

dinosaur

saddle

road

d d d d d d d · · · · · · · · · · · d

d d

d d

dad

add

dad dad

add add

2
+1
3

1 •
•2

•3

0 •

9 •
•4

8 •
•5

7 •
•6

duck

18

Ŏ Ŏ Ŏ Ŏ Ŏ Ŏ   · · ·   Ŏ

Ŏ   Ŏ

odd

odd
odd

odd

octopus   doctor   owl

0 •   • 9

1 •   • 8

3 •   • 6

2 •   • 7

4 • • 5

a goat 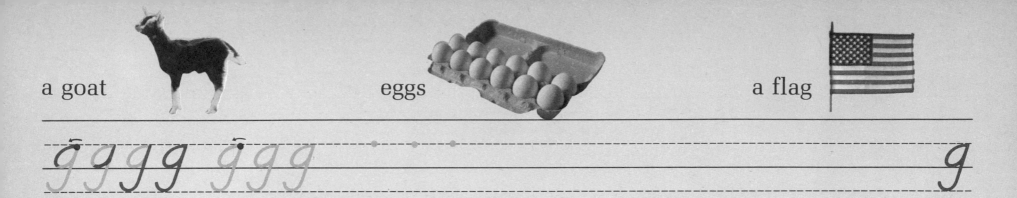 eggs a flag

ḡ ḡ ḡ ḡ   ḡ ḡ ḡ   g

go

a dog

a good dog

go   a dog   a good dog

g   g

D'Nealian Handwriting, Book 1. © Scott, Foresman and Company.

20

a cactus   a clown   a coconut   a cupcake

c c c   c c c   • • •   c

c   c

good cocoa

good cocoa

a dog

a dog

a cat

name

e e e e e e . . . e

e   e

an elephant

a wheel

a doe

a doe

a doe

egg

egg

D'Nealian Handwriting, Book 1. © Scott, Foresman and Company.

SUPERMARKET

S S S   S S   · · ·   *S*

S   *S*

a soda

a soda

gas

gas

a sad goose

a sad goose

a sailboat

name

cage

cages

egg

eggs

soda

sodas

dog

dogs

seed

seeds

dad

dads

D'Nealian Handwriting, Book 1. © Scott, Foresman and Company.

0 1 2 3 4 5 6 7 8 9 10

a fox

waffles

a leaf

f f f f f f f f f f   • • •   f

f   f

a safe

a safe

fog

fog

food

food

a face

a face

a sad face

a sad face

D'Nealian Handwriting, Book 1. © Scott, Foresman and Company.

b b b b b b   *b*

b   *b*

bees

bees

a bed

a bed

a badge

a badge

ℓ ℓ ℓ ℓℓℓ · · ·　　　　　　　　　　　ℓ
ℓ　　　　　　　　　　　　　　　　　ℓ

a leaf

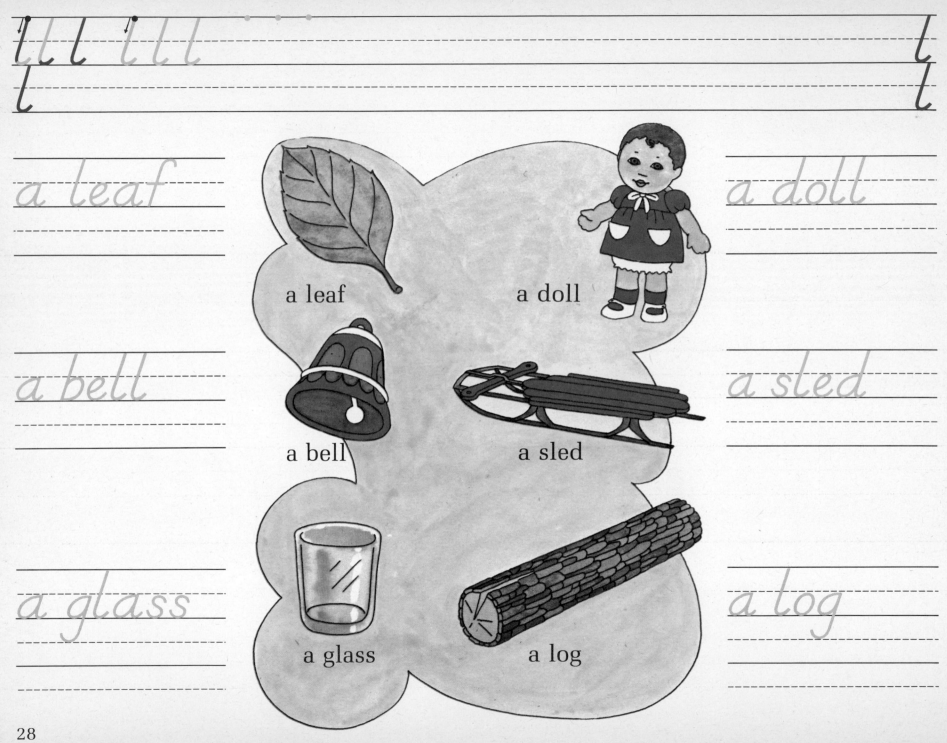

a leaf

a bell

a bell

a glass

a glass

a doll

a doll

a sled

a sled

a log

a log

28

D'Nealian Handwriting, Book 1. © Scott, Foresman and Company.

a tiger

mittens

a rabbit

t t t t tt ttt   t

t   t

a belt

a belt

a taco

a taco

bat

bat

a fat toad

a fat toad

name

29

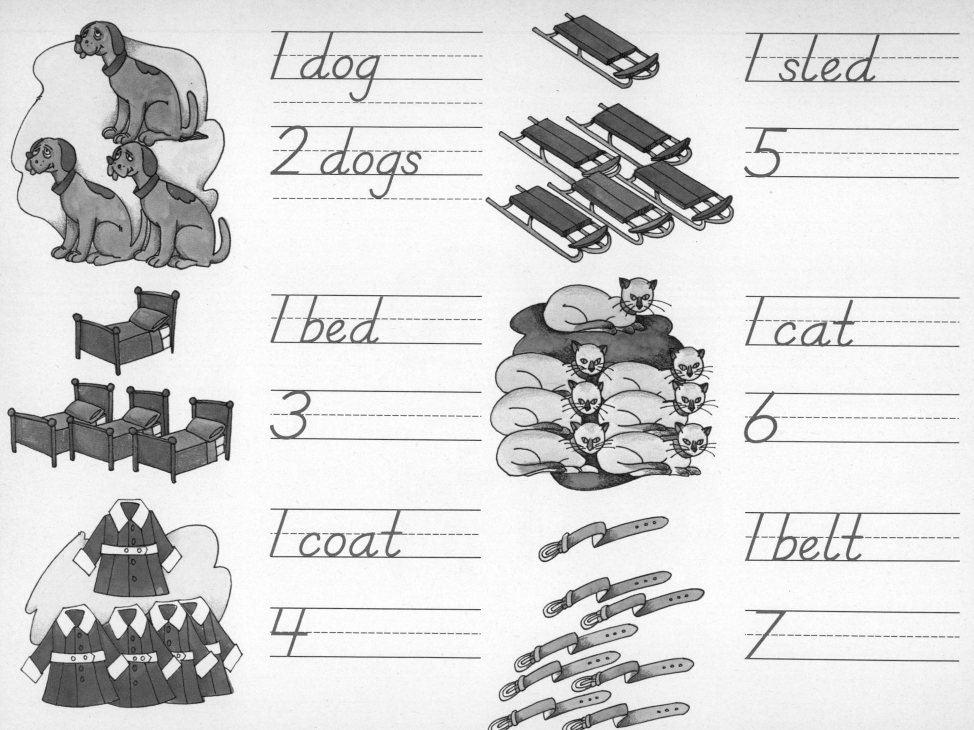

1 dog

2 dogs

1 bed

3

1 coat

4

1 sled

5

1 cat

6

1 belt

7

D'Nealian Handwriting, Book 1. © Scott, Foresman and Company.

a helicopter

a birdhouse

a brush

h h h h h h h   *h*

h   *h*

teeth

teeth

a hot dog

a hot dog

a hat

a hat

a ghost

a ghost

name

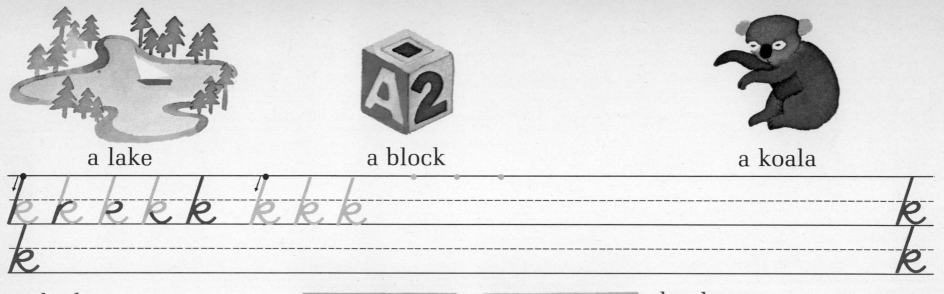

a lake   a block   a koala

k k k k k k k k   *k*

k   *k*

a clock

a clock

books

books

black socks

black socks

D'Nealian Handwriting, Book 1. © Scott, Foresman and Company.

cdhlot

hot
_____
- - - - - - - - - - - - - -
_____

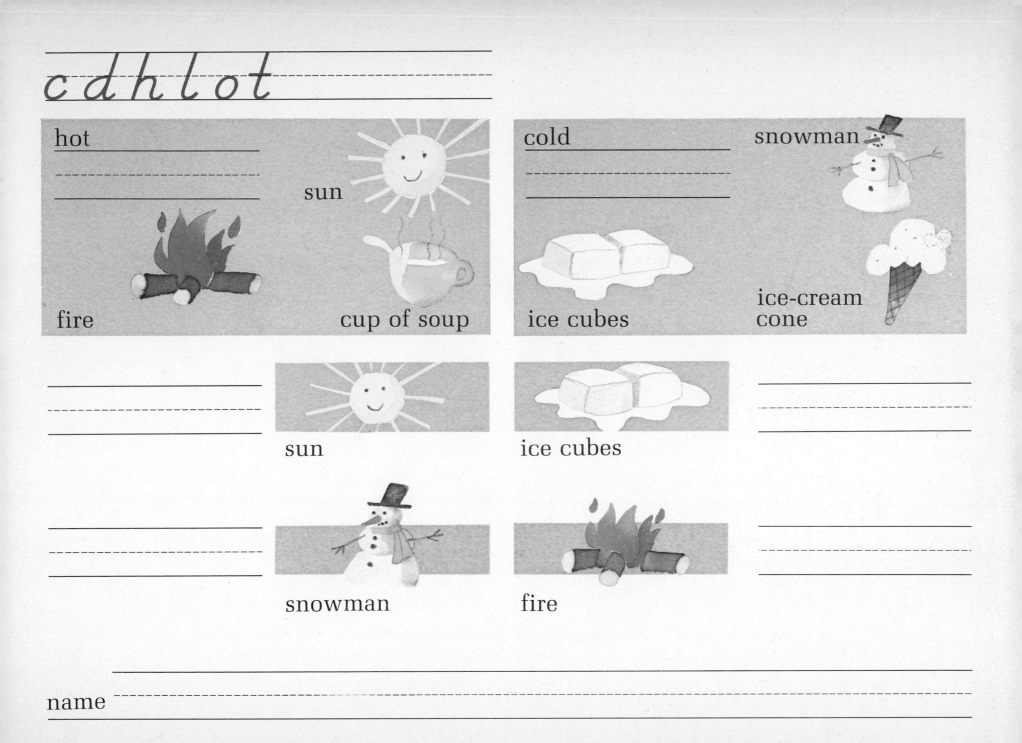

sun

fire

cup of soup

cold
- - - - - - - - - - - - - -
_____

snowman

ice cubes

ice-cream
cone

_____
- - - - - - - - - - - - - -
_____

sun

ice cubes

_____
- - - - - - - - - - - - - -
_____

_____
- - - - - - - - - - - - - -
_____

snowman

fire

_____
- - - - - - - - - - - - - -
_____

name

hat

hat

cake

cake

bell

bell

clock

clock

shoes

shoes

D'Nealian Handwriting, Book 1. © Scott, Foresman and Company.

i *i* *i* *i* *i* *i*   *i*

i   *i*

big

big

little

little

u u u u u u u u

u u

1.
house

2.
slide

3.
bus

4.
kite

5.
duck

2.

3.

5.

1.

1.

4.

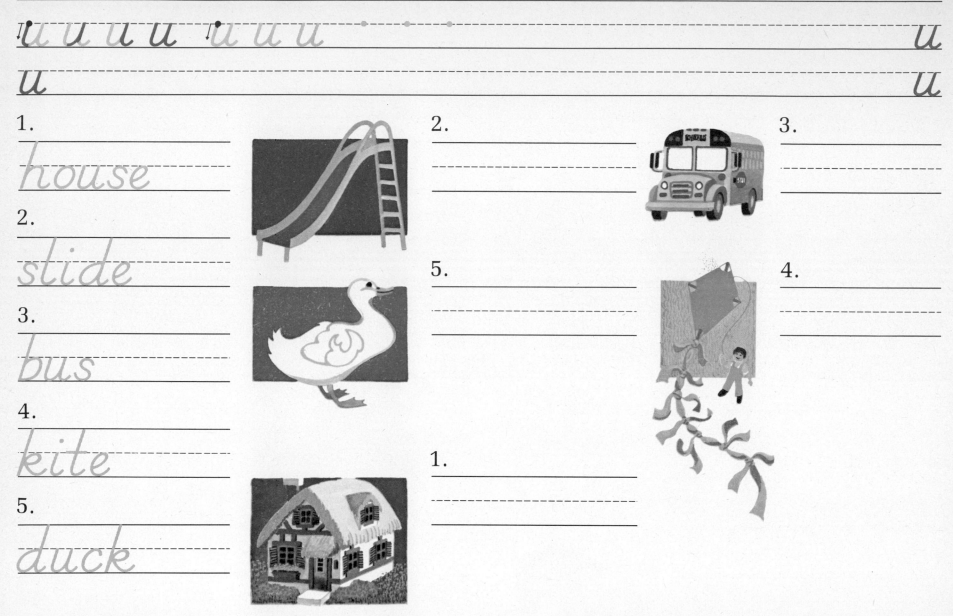

D'Nealian Handwriting, Book 1. © Scott, Foresman and Company.

name

windows

flowers

a cow

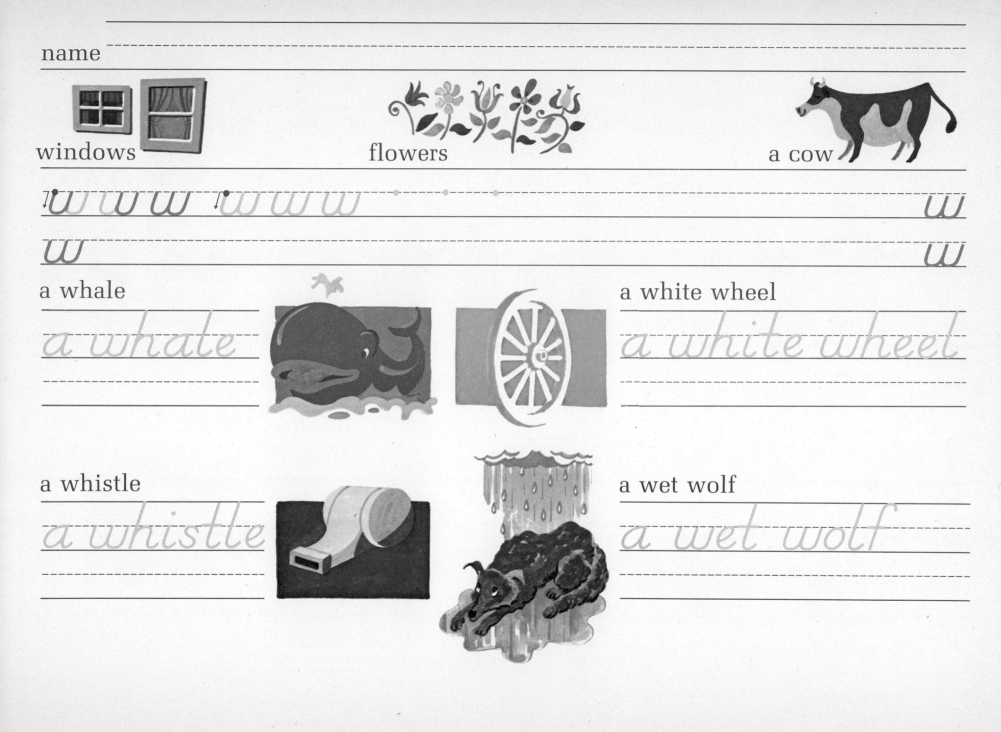

w w w w w w w   w
w   w

a whale

a whale

a white wheel

a white wheel

a whistle

a whistle

a wet wolf

a wet wolf

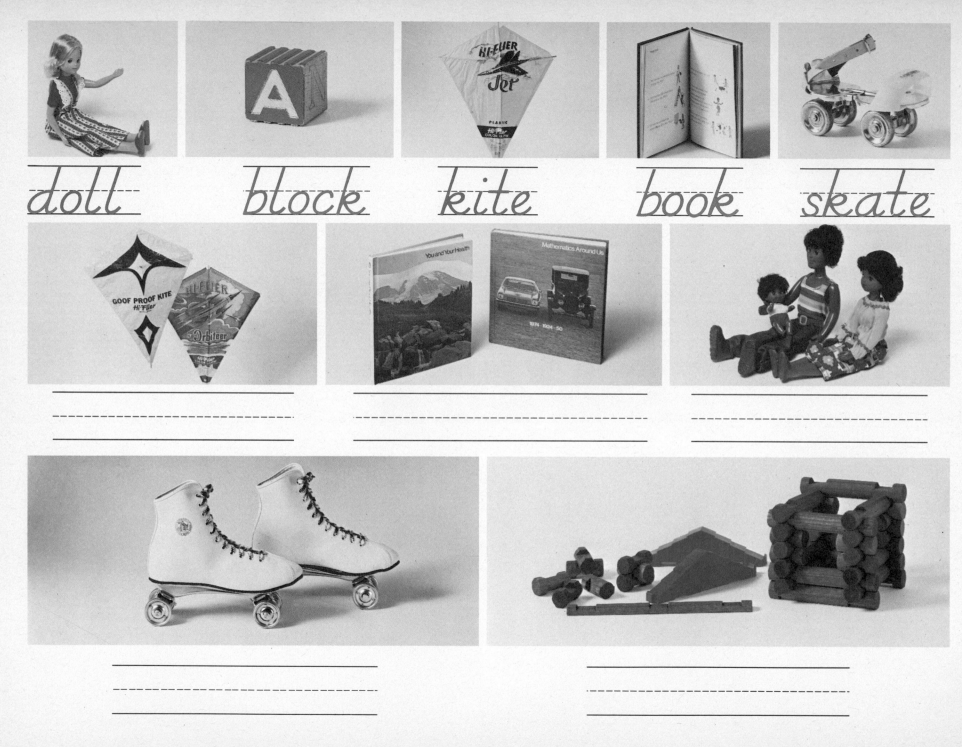

doll   block   kite   book   skate

a yard

a crayon

a butterfly

yyy yyy   y

a yoyo

a boy

a yellow toy

a yoyo   a boy   a yellow toy

y   y

name

jeans

pajamas

a blue jay

j j j j j j j j j j   *j*

jacks

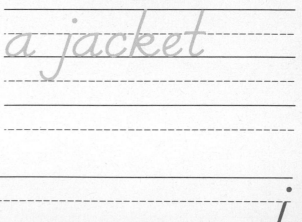

jelly

a jacket

jacks   *jelly*   *a jacket*

j   *j*

D'Nealian Handwriting, Book 1. © Scott, Foresman and Company.

a raccoon   an orange   a dinosaur

r r r r r r   r

r   r

a carrot

a carrot

red cherries

red cherries

a fork

a fork

a feather

a feather

four roosters

four roosters

D'Nealian Handwriting, Book 1. © Scott, Foresman and Company.

n n n n n n   *n*

n   *n*

two friends

two friends

four friends

four friends

d e f i l n o r s t

lots of friends

my friend

43

m m m m m m m   m

m   m

mouse   woman   museum   man

mouse   woman   museum   man

a c e h l m o r

1. hammer

3. home

2. camel

1.

2.

3.

D'Nealian Handwriting, Book 1. © Scott, Foresman and Company.

a penguin

a hippopotamus

a sheep

p p p p p p p   p

p   p

guppies

puppies

guppies   puppies

45

red   blue   brown   black
orange   yellow   purple   green

46

a queen

a square

an aquarium

q q q q q q q

q

q

a squirrel

a squirrel

a quart of milk

a quart of milk

a quilt

V V V V V V · · · V

V V

seven doves

seven doves

vases

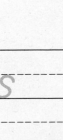

vases

five beavers

five beavers

a van

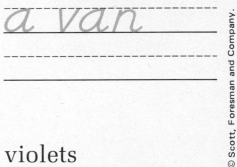

a van

vegetables

vegetables

violets

violets

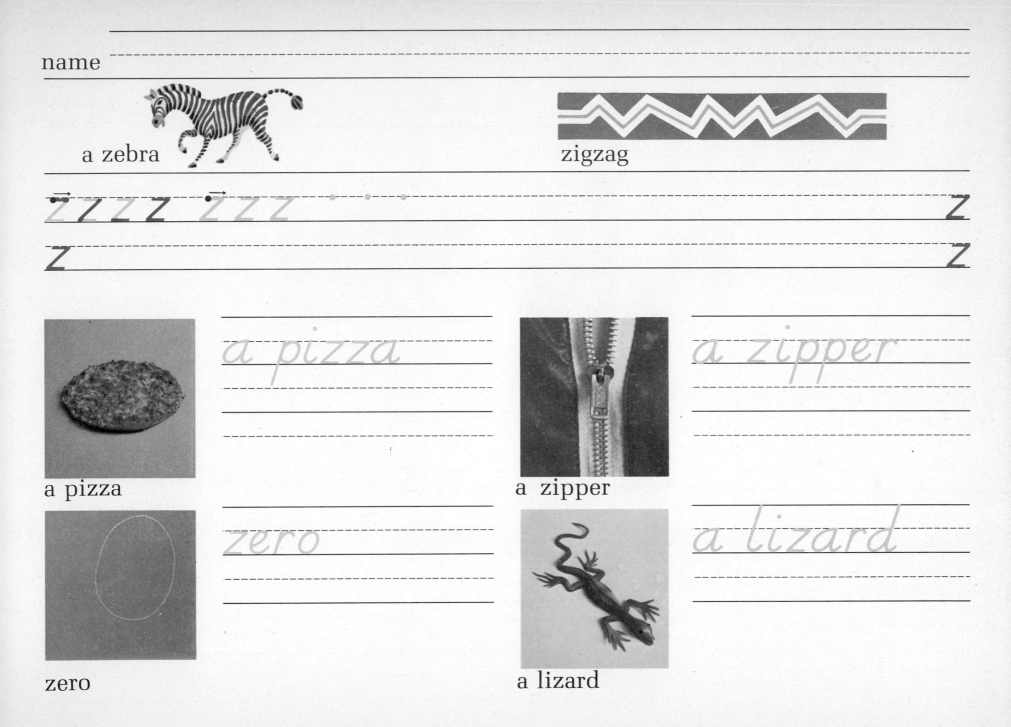

a zebra

zigzag

Z Z Z Z Z Z Z · · ·   Z

Z   Z

a pizza

a pizza

a zipper

a zipper

zero

zero

a lizard

a lizard

x x x x x x · · ·   x

x   x

six men

six men

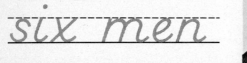

a fox

a fox

first   *last*   *next*

D'Nealian Handwriting, Book 1. © Scott, Foresman and Company.

a b c d e f g h i j k l m

n o p q r s t u v w x y z

a red fish

a red fish

blue socks

blue socks

an orange toy

an orange toy

a jump rope

a jump rope

51

0 1 2 3 4 5 6 7 8 9 10

zero

one

two

three

four

five

six

seven

eight

nine

ten

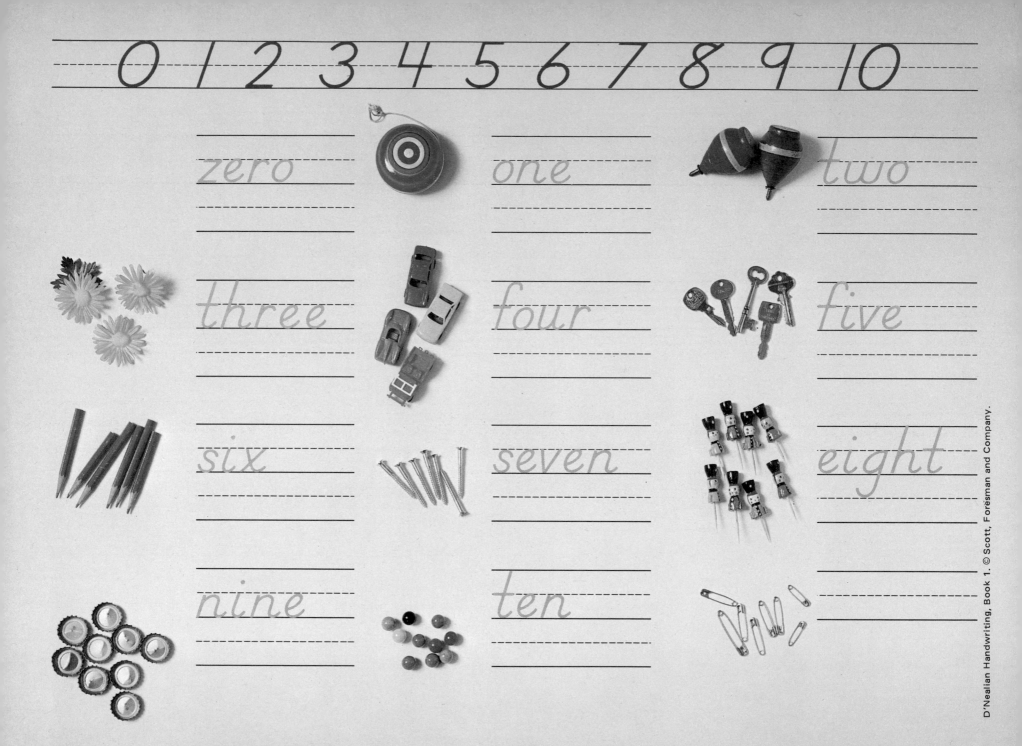

a d e f g h l m n o r t

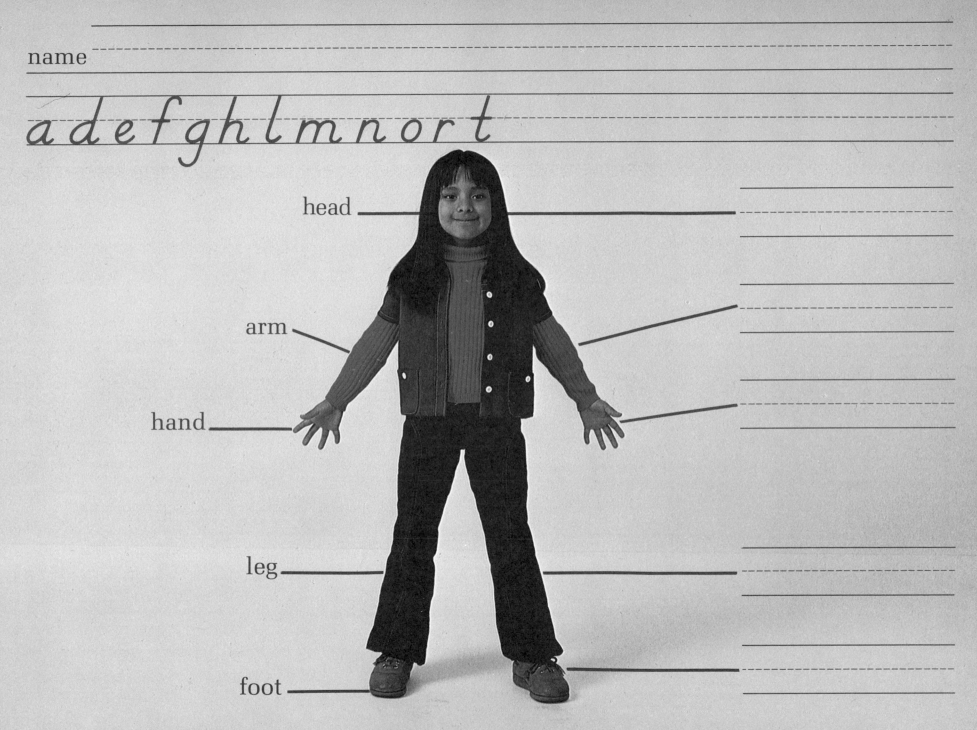

head

arm

hand

leg

foot

hippopotamus

hippopotamus

bee

bee

bear

bear

mouse

mouse

elephant

elephant

frog

frog

big

little

D'Nealian Handwriting, Book 1. © Scott, Foresman and Company.

name

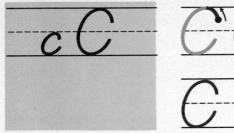 c C  C C C C C C · · · C

C C

Carole

Carole

Carlton

Carlton

Cecilia

Cecilia

Chris

Chris

Chico

Chico

Chuck

Chuck

55

g G   G G G   G G G   · · ·   G
G   G

George

George

Gigi

Gigi

George and Gigi

George and Gigi

Greg

Greg

Ginger

Ginger

Ginger and Greg

Ginger and Greg

D'Nealian Handwriting, Book 1. © Scott, Foresman and Company.

Giraffes are big animals.

Giraffes are big animals.

Camels are big too.

Camels are big too.

Caterpillars are little.

Caterpillars are little.

oO   OOO OOO   O

O   O

Oscar
Oscar

Ophelia
Ophelia

Ophelia likes oranges.
Ophelia likes oranges.

Oscar likes them too.
Oscar likes them too.

D'Nealian Handwriting, Book 1. © Scott, Foresman and Company.

q Q

Q Q Q Q Q Q Q Q

Q Q

Quack

Quack

Quilts keep you warm.

Quilts keep you warm.

name

s S

S S S S S S

S

S

Sue owns a bookstore.

Sue owns a bookstore.

She sells books.

She sells books.

D'Nealian Handwriting, Book 1. © Scott, Foresman and C

CGOQSadefghilmorstuw

Old Clothes

Garage Sale

Quilts for Sale

1. _____

2. _____

3. _____

Ivan likes to read.
I like to read too.

i I

I am a _____.

I go to school.

I like to _____.

girl

boy

school

read

play

D'Nealian Handwriting, Book 1. © Scott, Foresman and Company.

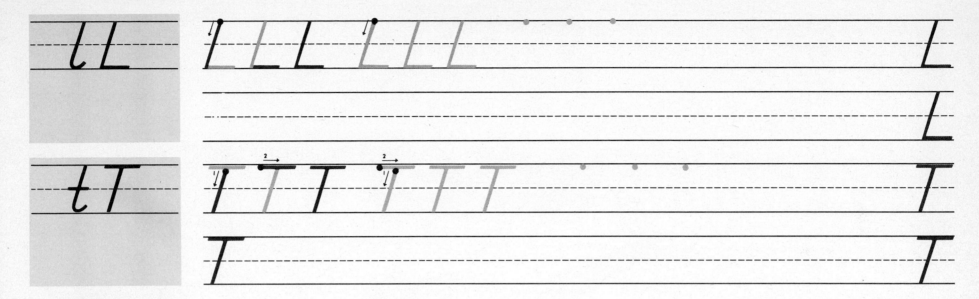

Linda lives in Louisiana.

Linda lives in Louisiana.

Trent lives in Tennessee.

Lana Leopard

Tina Tiger

Lisa Ladybug

Silly Skunk

Gina Giraffe

Sam Snake

stripes

spots

D'Nealian Handwriting, Book 1. © Scott, Foresman and Company.

j J

J J J J J J J

J

J

J

u U

U U U U U U

U

U

U

Uncle Jack

Uncle Jack

Uncle Jack uses a jeep.

Uncle Jack uses a jeep.

h H

H H

H H

k K

K K

K K

aehiknrtuy

Kent   Helen   Henry   Kiku

Kickball   Hopscotch

D'Nealian Handwriting, Book 1. © Scott, Foresman and Company.

name _____

HIJKLTU

Tamika

Igor

Kevin

Ursula

Lottie

Jane

Harold

a A

A A A A A A A A A A A A A A

A A

a h i l m n o p q r s t u w

Airport

Aquarium

Art Show

Animals

D'Nealian Handwriting, Book 1. © Scott, Foresman and Company.

b B

B B B B B   B B B   B

B   B

B G T a b c e h l m n o s u w

DDDD DDD D

D D

Doctor Dodge

Doctor Dodge

Doctor Dodge is
a dentist.

*Doctor Dodge is
a dentist.*

She fixes teeth.

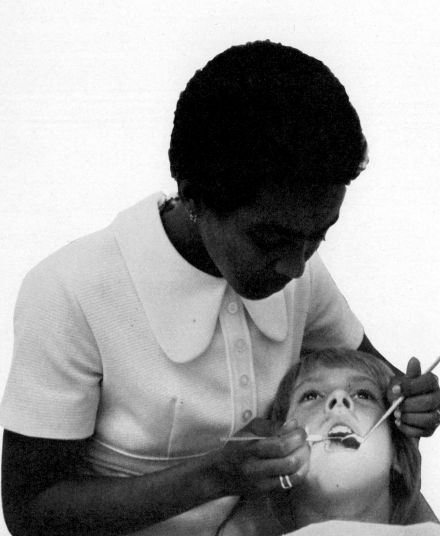

mM

MMMM MMM M

M M

Ms. Mertz

Ms. Mertz

Mrs. Miko

Mrs. Miko

Mr. Moreno

Mr. Moreno

Miss Mantom

Miss Mantom

Elmwood School's Favorite Snacks

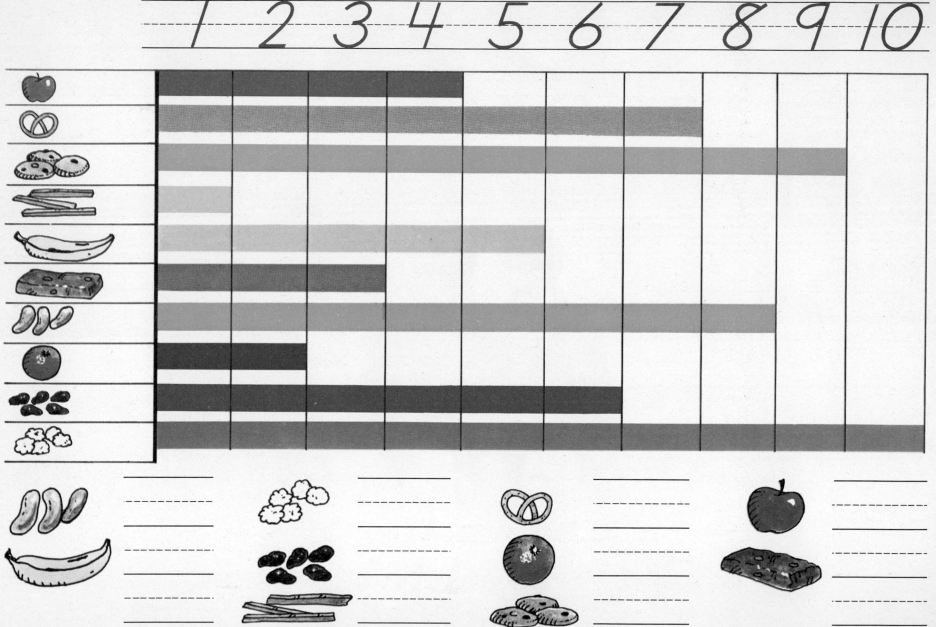

D'Nealian Handwriting, Book 1. © Scott, Foresman and Company.

CEREAL

MILK

Todd's
Grocery List
3 carrots
7 oranges
eggs

Bev's
Grocery List
2 pies
cereal
milk
10 apples

My Grocery List

n N N N N N N N N N

N N N

Neighborhood News

Neal has a baby sister.

Nora has a new tooth.

My News

D'Nealian Handwriting, Book 1. © Scott, Foresman and Company.

pP

P P P P P P P P   P

P   P

rR

R R R R R R R R   R

R   R

a c d h i k m n o p r s t u

Pumpkin Patch

Popcorn Rock

Radish Road

Pepper Rabbit

1.

2.

3.

ABDMNPR abcdehilmnotvy

Nancy

Michelle

Paco

Amanda

Reva

Don

Anthony

Bob

red

_____

green

_____

76

D'Nealian Handwriting, Book 1. © Scott, Foresman and Company.

name

e E

E

E

E

BDHIKLNOPRSTU

NO BIKES

KEEP OUT

ENTER HERE

DO NOT ENTER

Family Night Every Friday

f F

F

F

Fish

Fish

Fruit

Fruit

Beef

Beef

French Fries

French Fries

Food

D'Nealian Handwriting, Book 1. © Scott, Foresman and Company.

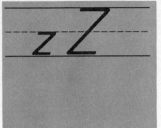

z Z

ZZZZ ZZZ   Z

Z   Z

Zachary likes to
visit the zoo.

Zachary likes to
visit the zoo.

Zebras make him dizzy.

Zebras make him dizzy.

Vivian likes movies.

Vivian likes movies.

Vernon likes TV.

Vernon likes TV.

Which one do you like best?

D'Nealian Handwriting, Book 1. © Scott, Foresman and Company.

name

Walt

Walt

Wanda

Wanda

Willie

Willie

Who is in the car?

Who is on the swing?

Who is skating?

Who is jumping?

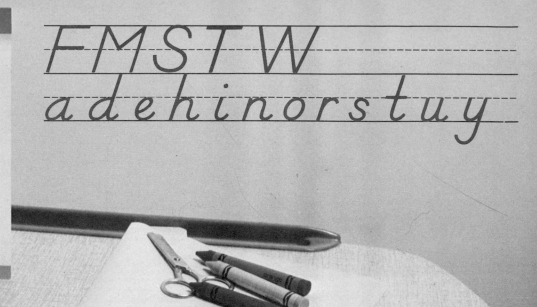

FMSTW
adehinorstuy

Sunday

Monday

Tuesday

Wednesday

Thursday

Friday

Saturday

D'Nealian Handwriting, Book 1. © Scott, Foresman and Company.

x X

y Y

Yoshio looks at X rays.

He sees bones in them.

bdfhklt

aceimnorsuvwxz

gjpqy

1. s s

2. a a

3. r r

4. d d

5. k k

6. b b

7. t t

8. c e

D'Nealian Handwriting, Book 1. © Scott, Foresman and Company.

A   G   L   Q

W   O   M   B   V

X   H   S   I   Z

C   Y   D   J   N

T   R   F   K

E   P   U

b

r

j

x

w

i

f

y

k

c

p

l

g

v

a

n

e

m

s

t

z

d

o

h

u

q

D'Nealian Handwriting, Book 1. © Scott, Foresman and Company.

melvin likes cars

he works hard

he wants to be a mechanic

a doctor | a cook | a teacher | a barber | a writer

What do you want to be?

Who are you?　　How are you?　　Where are you?

? ? ? ? ? ? ? ? ?

What kind of key will
not open doors?

a monkey　　a door key

Riddle from *A Pack of Riddles* compiled by William R. Gerler.
Text copyright © 1975 by William R. Gerler. Reprinted by permission of the publisher, E. P. Dutton and Co., Inc.

name

I am an animal.
My name begins with g.
What am I?

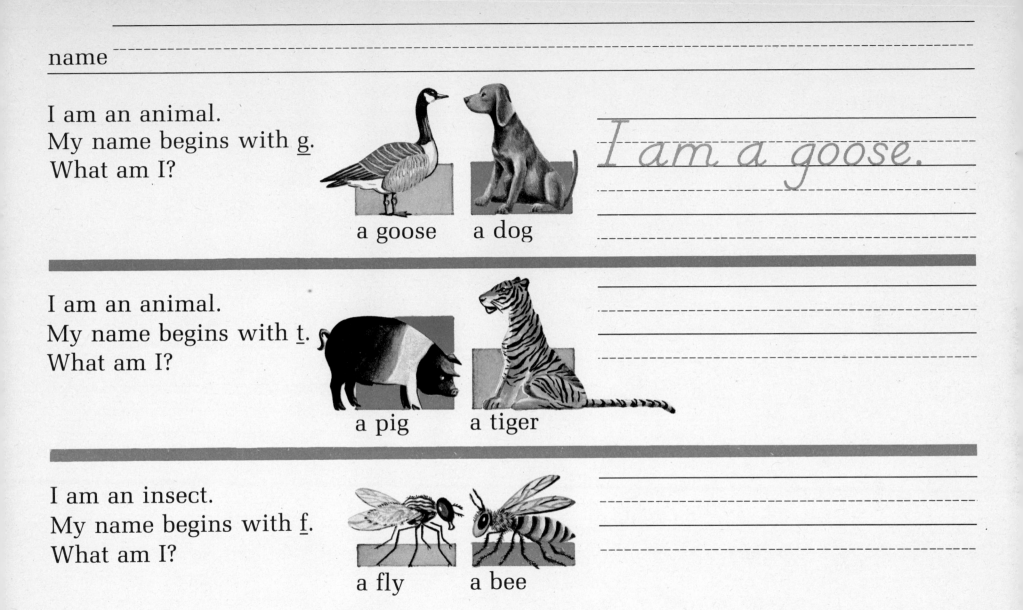

a goose   a dog

I am a goose.

I am an animal.
My name begins with t.
What am I?

a pig   a tiger

I am an insect.
My name begins with f.
What am I?

a fly   a bee

Pussy Feet

My kitty makes
No noise because
She walks around
On velvet paws.

"Pussy Feet" by Ruth Chandler from *Child Life* magazine, copyright © 1967 by Review Publishing Company, Inc., Indianapolis, Indiana 46206.

D'Nealian Handwriting, Book 1. © Scott, Foresman and Company.

bus
buses

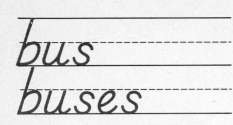

dress

fox

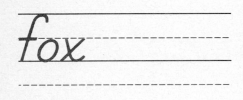

box
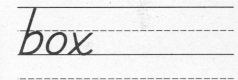

bench

watch

Anna's Family

Anna

brother

sister

cousin

Anna

brother

sister

cousin

mother

father

aunt

uncle

mother

father

aunt

uncle

grandmother

grandfather

grandmother

grandfather

My Family

D'Nealian Handwriting, Book 1. © Scott, Foresman and Company.

Tom   hat   Tom's hat   Mary   wagon   Mary's wagon

Tom's hat   *Mary's wagon*

Vicki   sled   Vicki's sled   *Vicki's sled*

Juan   radio   Juan's radio   *Juan's radio*

Queta   ring   Queta's ring   Queta's ring

a wig

a pig

a wig on a pig

a wig on a pig

a coat

a goat

a bee

a tree

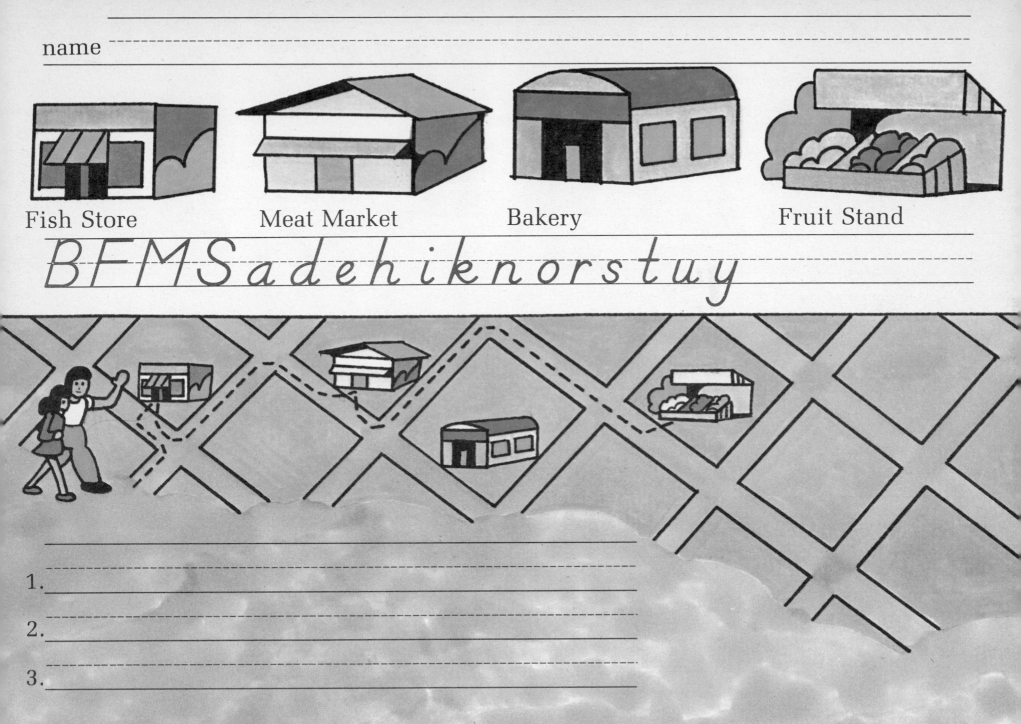

Fish Store   Meat Market   Bakery   Fruit Stand

BFMSadehiknorstuy

1.

2.

3.

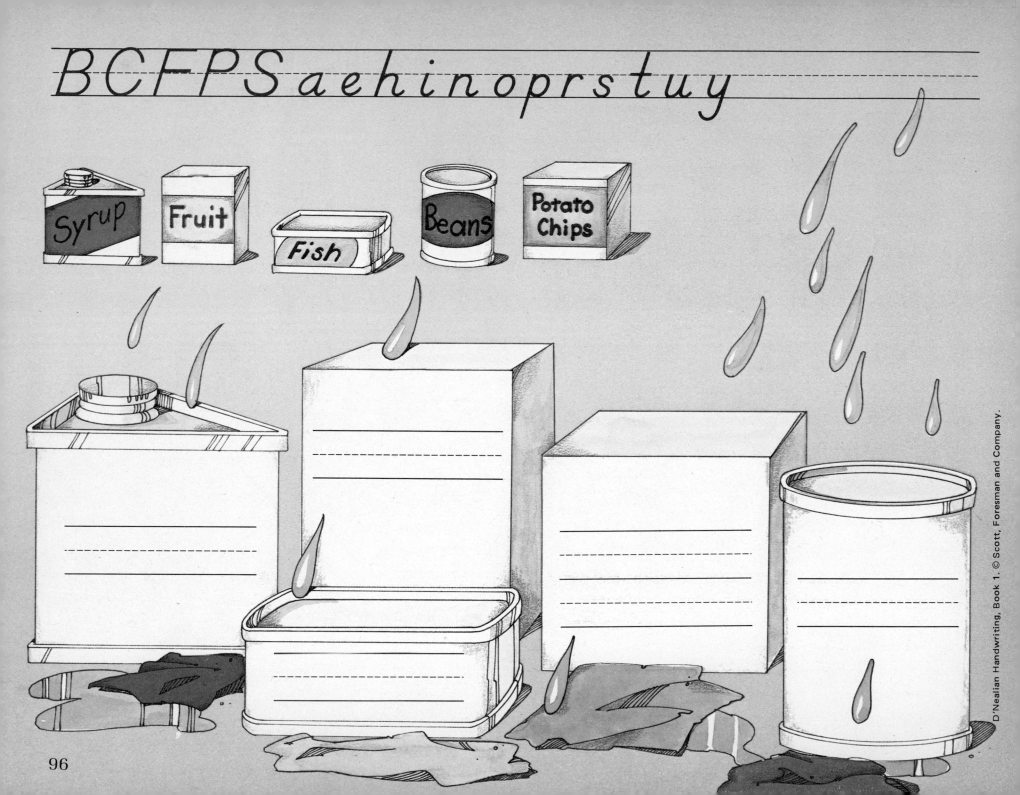

BCFPSaehinoprstuy

Syrup Fruit Fish Beans Potato Chips

D'Nealian Handwriting, Book 1. © Scott, Foresman and Company.

Christopher   Hannah Dee   Michiko

Raymond   Angela   Paul

hot dogs   rolls   apple

popcorn   carrots   milk

What will you bring?

 sunny

 cloudy

 rainy

snowy

rainy

D'Nealian Handwriting, Book 1. © Scott, Foresman and Company.

beside

under

above   over

between

in

behind

Where is the bird?

beside a tree

CGOQSacdeghil
mnoqrstuvwy

Quentin | sandwiches

Olivia | quilts

Gordon | candy

Sandy | oranges

Carla | gum

Quentin has quilts.

Quentin has quilts.

Olivia has oranges.

Gordon has gum.

Sandy has sandwiches.

Carla has candy.

D'Nealian Handwriting, Book 1. © Scott, Foresman and Company.

 Susan  Phil  April  David  Kim  Jody  Fred  Rick

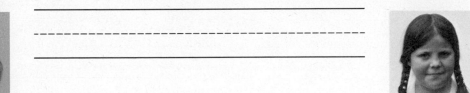

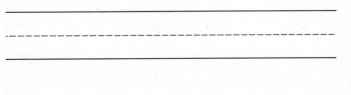

Free
Is being able
To
Jump
Without falling.

_____

- - - - - - - - - - - - - - - - -

_____

- - - - - - - - - - - - - - - - -

_____

- - - - - - - - - - - - - - - - -

_____

"Free" by Ginger Allen from *Poetry in the Schools North Carolina* 1972 edited by
Ardis Kimzey, Copyright © 1972 by North Carolina Department of Public Instruction.
Reprinted by permission.

D'Nealian Handwriting, Book 1. © Scott, Foresman and Company.

a b c d e f g h i j k l m
n o p q r s t u v w x y z

O R U Q S V P W

A F I C K M L G

N Y D E H J T B

name

wet   dry   hard   soft   happy   sad   up   down

happy

sad

name

105

a b c d e f g h i j k l m
n o p q r s t u v w x y z

green   blue   yellow   red   black   orange

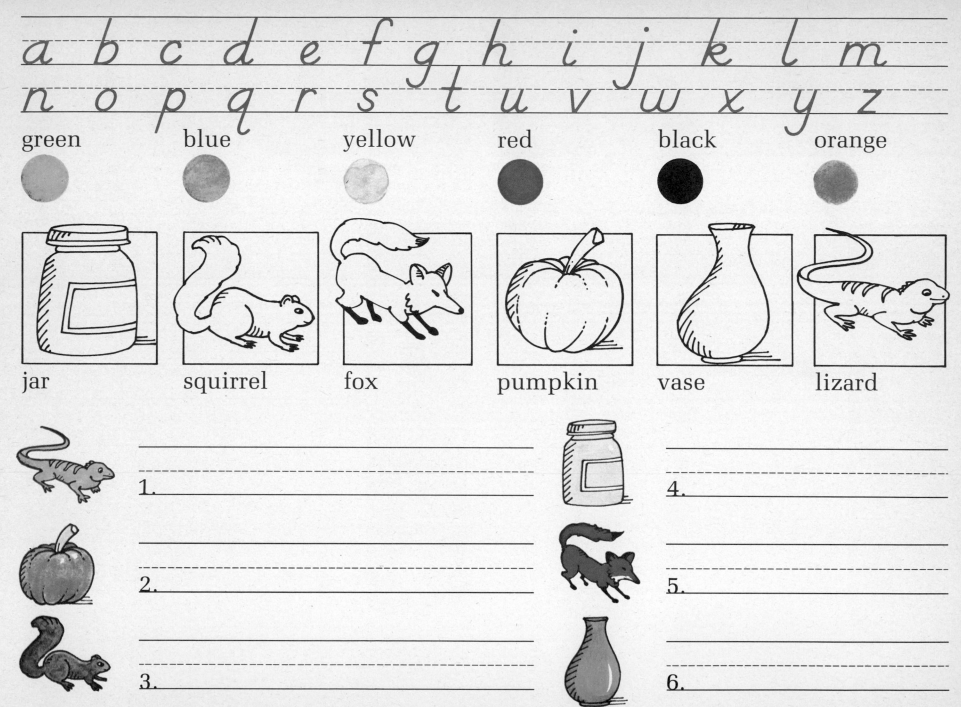

jar   squirrel   fox   pumpkin   vase   lizard

1.

2.

3.

4.

5.

6.

D'Nealian Handwriting, Book 1. © Scott, Foresman and Company.

2   *A*   *B*   *C*

3

4

5

6

7

8

9

name

_____ _____ _____ , _____ _____ _____ ? _____

It is dark outside.
Jo's bike is in the yard.
Can you see the bike?

My Page

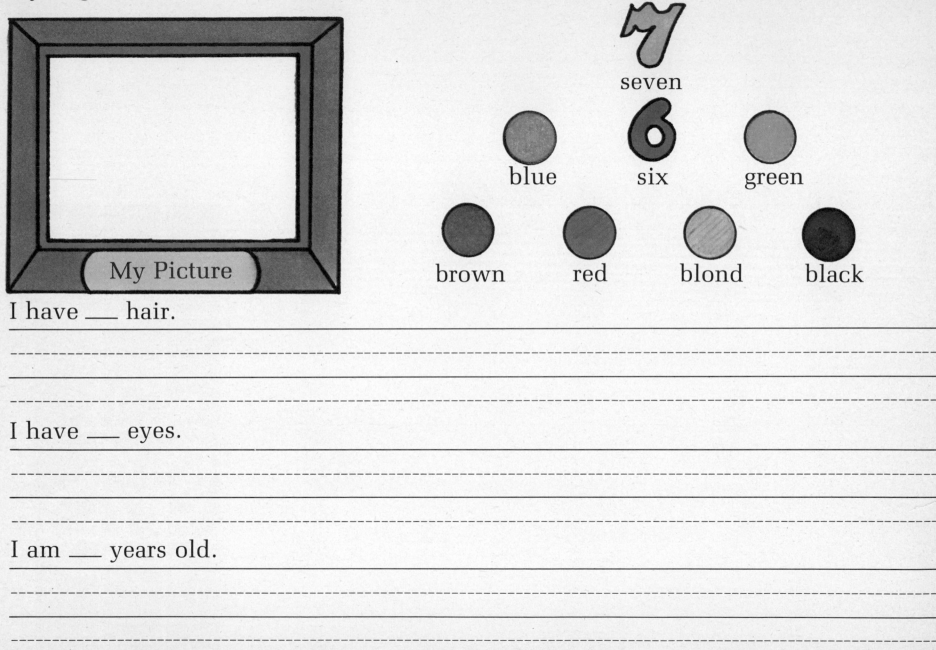

My Picture

seven

blue   six   green

brown   red   blond   black

I have ___ hair.

I have ___ eyes.

I am ___ years old.

D'Nealian Handwriting, Book 1. © Scott, Foresman and Company.